Contents

Should You Take Your Dog?

Dogs have been traveling with people for thousands of years. They accompanied them across the Bering land bridge from Asia to the Americas some 10,000 to 15,000 years ago; indeed, without dogs to pull heavy objects and warn of predators, people might not have survived the arduous journey. Later, traders from the Phoenicians onward carried various types of dogs from port to port, exchanging them along the way for other goods. Toy dogs accompanied great ladies wherever they went, and war

dogs accompanied the Romans as they marched through Britain some 2,000 years ago.

Today, we still enjoy having our dogs with us when we travel. A dog is a little bit of home in a sterile hotel room, a friend in a sea of strangers, a watchful eye and an alert ear in an unfamiliar place. Having a dog on a trip is a great way to meet new people.

While moving to a new home is a trip that must include the family dog, people are also choosing to take their pets along when they vacation. Today hotels and resorts are more readily welcoming four-footed travelers. Consider

taking Bianca on vacation with you if she's healthy, adaptable, well behaved, and enjoys new places and new people.

Don't take your pooch if you can't spend time with her, however. Don't take her on a business trip if you'll be tied up in meetings or making sales calls all day. *Do* take her when the two of you can lounge on a beach, swim in a lake, or explore a new city together.

This book covers the practical planning that goes into taking a dog on a trip, whether it's a one-day car ride to a new home, a one-week vacation, or a one-year sojourn

overseas. You'll learn how to find dog-friendly accommodations, how to pack for your dog, how to arrange air
travel, how to find a veterinarian in a strange city, and
proper travel etiquette. Happy trails!

Places To Go, Things To Do

Resourceful pet owners can make almost any trip dog friendly, but certain activities and places have special allure. The great outdoors is always a draw. Whether large or small, active or laidback, most dogs enjoy the scents and sounds found on hiking trails and beaches.

Camping and boating are wonderful activities to share with your dog. Yet cities hold many of the same attractions (on a different level)—good things to smell (and eat!), birds to chase, and open spaces (parks) to play in.

Dog-loving entrepreneurs have created camps for dogs and their people and trips designed to allow dogs to participate. At dog camps, you and Buster can try out dog sports such as agility, flyball, herding, and tracking. You can learn animal communication skills and clicker training or study canine nutrition and holistic health care. Buster can learn tricks and acting skills. Dogcentric tours include river rafting in Colorado; houseboating on Lake Powell in Utah; canoeing in Canada; and touring Santa Barbara, California—including a botanical garden, a beach barbecue, and a ride in a self-powered quadricycle. To be wel-

come at a camp or on a tour, your pooch needs only a

friendly attitude toward other dogs and people.

Dog-friendly cities include San Francisco; New York;

Paris; Chicago; Seattle; Toronto; Vancouver; and Washington, D.C. It's easy to see these cities on foot, taking rest stops at cafés with outdoor seating and detours into  department stores, such as Macy's and Bloomingdales, whose salespeople don't bat an eye at canine customers. When you get tired of walking, hop on the dog-friendly public transportation in some of these cities.

Many European countries have an enlightened attitude toward dogs in public. You'll see dogs in restaurants and shops and on subways and trains in France, Germany, Austria, and Switzerland. Check the rules before you ride; Buster may need to be leashed and sometimes muzzled.

Cities are also great because they have parks. Chicago has eighteen miles of trails along the shores of Lake Michigan. Other favorites include New York's Central Park, San Francisco's Crissy Field and Baker Beach, and Vancouver's 1,000-acre Stanley Park. In Washington, D.C., jog with Buster through Rock Creek Park or a walk on the

National Mall, stopping at the memorial of dog-loving president Franklin D. Roosevelt. If you and Buster are baseball fans, you can attend one of the annual Dog Days games held by teams in many cities. (You'll need a special ticket.)

Other good areas include Cape Cod and Nantucket in Massachusetts; Carmel, Monterey, Laguna Beach, and Lake Tahoe in California; and Key West, Florida. Each has plenty of dog-friendly lodgings.

Nantucket Airlines and the island's ferry system transport dogs, as do the island's shuttle buses. Leashed dogs can romp at Cape Cod National Seashore; in California, dogs can run off leash at Carmel City Beach. Dogs are everywhere in Laguna, from the boardwalk on Main Beach to the shops and the dining patios of places such as the Ocean Avenue Brewery. Up Pacific Coast Highway in Newport Beach is the dog-friendly shopping center Fashion Island. Outdoorsy types can take dogs river rafting at Lake Tahoe or on a gondola ride up the mountain at Squaw Valley. Florida's Key West Aquarium permits well-behaved dogs (keep your canine out of the shark tanks).

Taking your dog to Yosemite, Yellowstone, and other great national parks is not so easy. Most restrict dogs to

paved trails, require them to be leashed (always a good idea, wherever you are), and don't permit them at park lodges.

If you want to hike or camp in the backcountry, consider national forests with fewer developed areas and fewer restrictions. You can get an experience similar to that in Yellowstone's backcountry at the nearby Custer or Gallatin National Forests.

Wherever you and Buster decide to go, plan carefully to ensure a successful trip. Read on to see what to pack and how to make reservations.

Finding a Hotel

You need to find places that will welcome Bianca. Even if you're only going tent or RV camping, you need to call ahead to make sure the campsite permits dogs. Ask about restrictions, such as number of pets, leash rules, and quiet hours.

If you're planning a hotel stay, options range from the plainest roadside motels to the poshest hotel. To find hotels and motels that welcome dogs, start with an Internet search at Web sites such as http://www.petswel-

come.com and http://www.petsonthego.com. These sites and others will help you find the right place. You can also try one of the many books listing pet-friendly lodgings, but make sure you're looking at a recent one.

Among the pet-friendly hotel and motel chains are Starwood (comprising Westin, Sheraton, and W hotels), Loews, Kimpton, Marriott, Ritz-Carlton, Four Seasons, Days Inn, Embassy Suites, Red Roof Inn, Best Western, and Motel 6. Resorts permitting dogs include San Ysidro Ranch in Montecito, California; the St. Regis Monarch Beach Resort in Dana Point, California; and Green Valley Spa in St.

George, Utah. Many upscale hotels not only permit dogs but also cater to them. Starwood hotels offer canine guests beds, food and water bowls, ID tags, and treats. At Loews hotels, your dog will receive a welcome gift of food and water bowls with a place mat, toys, treats, and a note from the manager with information on places to walk your dog and local services.

When you've found a place you're interested in, confirm the pet policy before making a reservation. Policies change often and can vary from hotel to hotel, even within a chain. For instance, the Ritz-Carlton in Chicago

gives dogs the royal treatment, but the Ritz-Carlton in Dana Point, California, does not permit them. Note whom you spoke to in case of confusion at check in. If the hotel's corporate Web site (not the chain's Web site) mentions that it allows pets, print that page and take it with you.

Ask about limitations on the number or size of dogs and

additional fees for your dog. Fees can range from $5 to $175 per dog or per stay and are not always refundable. They vary even among hotels that belong to the same chain. In the Starwood chain for instance, dogs stay free at Sheratons and Westins, but W hotels charge $25 per stay.

Be sure to request a first- or second-floor room when making reservations. That's more convenient for taking Bianca out to potty.

When you stay at any hotel or motel, follow a few rules of canine hotel etiquette to make sure you and Bianca, as well as other dogs and owners, will be welcomed back.

Crate her when you leave her in the room. Even the best-behaved dog can become destructive in a strange place. If you allow her on any furniture, cover it first with your own sheet or throw. Clean up any accidents immediately, and always dispose of her mess appropriately. Keep the noise down. If Bianca barks when left alone, take her with you when you leave the room.

Puppy Packing Protocol

Now you need to pack Buster's bag. Fill a tote bag with food and water dishes, food and treats, a measuring cup for dishing out kibble, grooming tools, plastic bags, a favorite toy or two, and an extra leash. For excursions along the way (or from your destination), bring a day pack to hold water bottles, a folding nylon water dish, plastic bags, and treats. It's also a good idea to pack a canine first-aid kit, which should include some Kaopectate, in case of stomach upset from excitement or a change in

water. Take your favorite enzymatic cleanser and some old towels to clean up any accidents as well.

Stash Buster's vaccination records in a side pocket of his bag in case you need to board him for a day. Keep a recent picture of him, too—you may need it for "lost" flyers if he becomes separated from you. Put an ID tag with your cell phone number on his collar.

You'll also need a crate and bedding. Any crate will do, as long as it fits in your car, but consider buying a lightweight, collapsible fabric model that's easy to set up and take down. You can also find plastic or wire crates that fold up when not in use. If Buster usually lounges on the furniture, take a large sheet to throw over the hotel bed so he doesn't leave hair on the bedspread.

Finally, find out where you can buy Buster's food along the way. If he eats a national-brand food widely available in grocery or pet supply stores, you're set; but if he eats a specialty brand, go to the company's Web site or call its toll-free number to get the names, phone numbers, and addresses of retailers along your route. Store the information with important paperwork. Now you're ready to hit the road.

On the Road

By car, van, or RV is probably the easiest and most fun way to travel with your dog. A good traveling companion, Bianca won't argue over the radio station or tell you that you could have been there already if you hadn't taken that wrong turn. She's a good excuse to take a break every couple of hours, and she's thrilled by all the exciting new scents at rest stops, canine Disneylands with no fees. The following tips will help your trip go smoothly.

First and foremost, teach Bianca to wait until you put

her leash on and give an OK before jumping out of the car. Otherwise, she could get hit by a car or run away.

Buy a canine seatbelt or car seat. A good seatbelt adjusts to fit Bianca comfortably and easily attaches to your car's seatbelt system. A soft lining, an adjustable strap to allow some movement, and a built-in leash for walks are pluses. If Bianca is small, look for a car seat that will allow her to see out the window yet keep her confined. It should attach to your car's seatbelt system and have straps that attach to Bianca's harness so she can't jump out of it. Some seats have drawers in the bottom for storing dishes or leashes. Whether they're restrained by a canine seatbelt or car seat, dogs should ride in the back seat to prevent injury in case of accident.

Prepare your car by spreading a beach towel, sheet, or car seat cover across the back seat to catch hair. Secure Bianca's crate on the seat so she can crawl in for a nap if she gets bored. Place a two-gallon jug of water where it will be easily accessible at rest stops. (Mix in the local water along the way so her stomach can slowly adjust.) Once everything is ready, load Bianca up, hook her into her seatbelt or car seat, and give her a favorite chew toy. If she tends to get carsick, make sure she can see out the window, and take ginger snaps to help relieve an upset tummy.

Taking Bianca with you in an RV is even easier than traveling by car because you can stop whenever and wherever you want. Many campgrounds and RV parks permit dogs, but it's always a good idea to check in advance if you want to stay at a particular place.

Keep Bianca crated or secured with her doggie seatbelt

while the RV is in motion. Place the crate in an area that doesn't get too hot and attach it to something permanently affixed. To protect walls and floors, use self-adhesive Velcro dots to attach a thin piece of plywood or similar material to the wall behind the crate and a plastic mat beneath it. Use carpet film—available from camping or RV supply stores—to protect floors.

To prevent spills, purchase a Buddy Bowl. Depending on the size you choose, it holds a quart to a half-gallon of water and won't spill, even if turned upside down.

Bring an exercise pen to set up outside when you stop, giving Bianca a safe place to hang out. If the campground has a dirt surface, use roll-up plastic blinds as a "floor" for the pen. They will keep Bianca off the ground and are easily hosed off and rolled up for storage.

Air Travel

Traveling with Buster by air is not as easy as a few years ago. New security regulations mean more time in the airport before boarding, as well as tighter restrictions on baggage—including dogs. It can be done, but it's more expensive and requires plenty of planning.

To find out about pet regulations, go to the airline's Web site and enter "pets" or "dogs" into the search function or call the airline's 800 number. Write down the name and title of the person with whom you speak, as well as

the date and time of the conversation and have that information with you at check in, in case there's a problem.

You'll need to make yours and Buster's reservations at the same time. Most airlines charge $75 to $100 each way for a dog in the cabin, even though he doesn't take up a seat. The airline may require a health certificate from your veterinarian, which usually must be dated within ten days of the trip.

When Buster is traveling in the cabin, his carrier, which can be soft or hard sided, must fit beneath the seat. He should be able to stand up and turn around inside it. The

maximum size for cabin pet carriers is 23 inches long, 13 inches wide, 9 inches high. American airlines typically do not allow dogs in the cabin on transatlantic or transpacific flights. If you're flying to a dog-friendly European country such as France or Germany, consider a European airline such as Air France, which permits dogs weighing 11 pounds or less to travel in the cabin on overseas flights.

Air travel to Hawaii or to certain foreign countries requires special planning. Dogs may face a four- to six-month quarantine period if they don't meet health requirements. These may include certain vaccinations, blood testing, and parasite treatments within a specified time, as well as microchip identification. For information on travel to Hawaii, contact the office of the Hawaii state veterinarian. For foreign travel, contact the appropriate embassy or consulate as far in advance as possible. It often takes four to six months to meet all the requirements.

In a perfect world, Buster would fly only in the cabin of the plane, accompanied by you. When his size precludes that, he can fly as checked baggage or cargo. Schedule a direct flight whenever possible.

He will need a hard-sided kennel with room to stand,

turn around, and lie down in. Choose one with handles for lifting and side rims preventing other cargo from blocking vents. Mark the kennel "Live Animal" on the top and side, with arrows to indicate the right side up.

On top of the kennel, securely attach a sealed plastic bag containing a small amount of dry dog food, an envelope with feeding and watering instructions, and your contact information in case Buster is delayed in transit. Feed him four hours before the flight, and make sure he has a chance to potty prior to check-in. Before the flight, freeze some water in his dish and place it in the crate

when he's checked in. He can lick the ice as it melts during the trip, making spills less likely.

When you check him in, have the health certificate from your veterinarian. Give the desk agent your pup's name; personalizing Buster makes it more likely the agent will pay special attention to him. If you're on the same flight as your dog, ask the gate agent when you board if he can check on Buster's status for you to ensure he's safely stowed.

Whether Buster travels in the cabin or the plane's belly, avoid giving him tranquilizers. Sedation affects a dog's equilibrium, and the increased altitude—even in a pres-

surized cargo bay—can cause respiratory and cardiovas-cular problems. This is of special concern with pugs, bull-dogs, or other flat-faced breeds.

If you don't want Buster in cargo, check out Companion Air. This animal-friendly airline, which flies jet-propelled aircraft out of small airports, has an area in the rear of the main cabin where pets of all sizes can ride in their crates and be visited by owners. Companion Air is best suited for people who are relocating and have a flexible schedule, as flight schedules are tentative until the airline books enough travelers to make the trip cost effective.

Life at Sea

Taking Bianca for a day of sailing or a long-term cruise can be fun as long as she's properly prepared. The following tips will help you turn a canine landlubber into a sea dog.

Spend a day or two aboard the boat while it's docked, letting Bianca explore at her own pace. Practice getting on and off the boat. She may balk at walking a gangplank or jumping onto a surface that rocks when she lands, so be patient and lure her with treats or a favorite toy. Praise her when she walks on confidently.

Limit your first trip to an hour or two. This shakedown cruise will help Bianca get her sea legs. If you find she's prone to seasickness or know from car rides that she suffers from motion sickness, ask your veterinarian to recommend an appropriate dose of Dramamine to be given before departure.

To keep Bianca from falling overboard, run a jack line along the boat's port and starboard (left and right) sides. Connect that line by a ring to a safety line attached to Bianca's harness. Once the line is secure, she can then wander without constant supervision. For additional safety, place netting between the stanchions (vertical poles or posts) all the way around the boat.

If she does go overboard, a canine life preserver will keep her afloat until you get to her. Choose one that fits snugly without restricting movement. It should be bright yellow or orange so it's easily seen. Other features should include adjustable straps, quick-release buckles, and a top handle for ease in hauling. If she takes a saltwater dip, rinse her with fresh water to prevent dry skin or irritation.

Don't forget to protect Bianca from sunburn, especially if she has a light-colored coat. A T-shirt can prevent burns. If

nothing else, apply sunscreen to her ears and nose, choosing one that's waterproof and safe if ingested (no PABA). You can find sunscreen that's specially formulated for dogs.

For a trip longer than a few hours, pack a duffle with food, dishes, and a favorite toy. Keep a no-spill water dish on board for Bianca. Have plastic bags for clean-up if you go ashore. The items in your personal first-aid kit—antibiotic ointment, bandages, Dramamine, and sunscreen—will work for Bianca as well. Make sure she wears a collar and tag with your name, the name of your boat, and your slip number.

Resources

Web sites come and go, but the following list should help you get started finding dog-friendly accommodations, camps, and other vacation opportunities; pet travel accessories, flight information, and requirements for traveling abroad. See you on the road!

http://www.Akc.org/life/family/vac_hols/travel_tips.cfm

http://www.Aphis.usda.gov/oa/pubs/petravel.html

http://www.Baileyknowstravel.com

http://www.Blueskydogsny.com

http://www.Campdogwood.com

http://camp-gone-tothe-dogs.com/

http://www.Campw.com

http://www.Canineauto.com

http://www.Companionair.com

http://www.Dogcamp.com

http://www.Dogfriendly.com

http://www.Dogpaddlingadventures.com

http://dogpark.com/

http://dogs.about.com/od/travel/

http://www.Dog-play.com

http://www.Dogscouts.com

http://www.Dogskillsadventure.com

http://www.Fidofriendly.com

http://www.Gateway.library.uiuc.edu/vex/cpl/faq/travel.htm

http://www.Iron-dogs.com

http://www.Nps.gov

http://www.Petfriendlytravel.com

Acknowledgments

Many dog lovers contributed their expertise and advice to this book, include Robert E. Armstrong, DVM, who travels with Charlie, a Yorkie mix; Alice Bixler, a judge and breeder-exhibitor of bearded collies; Saluki maven D. Caroline Coile, PhD; Norwegian elkhound owner Lexiann Grant-Snyder; Alaskan malamute breeder Charlene LaBelle; trainer and Australian Shepherd owner Liz Palika; and pet-care columnist and author of *Dogs for Dummies* Gina Spadafori, who travels with flatcoats and a sheltie.

Kim Campbell Thornton is an award-winning writer and editor. During her tenure as editor of *Dog Fancy*, the magazine won three Dog Writers Association of America Maxwell Awards for best all-breed magazine. Her book *Why Do Cats Do That?* was named best behavior book in 1997 by the Cat Writers Association. Kim is the author of *Barking*, *Chewing*, *Digging*, *House-Training*, and *Aggression*. She served on the DWAA Board of Governors and is also the former president of the Cat Writers Association.

Buck Jones's humorous illustrations have appeared in numerous magazines (including *Dog Fancy* and *Cat Fancy*) and books. He is the illustrator for the best-selling Simple Solutions series, *Why Do Cockatiels Do That?*, *Why Do Parakeets Do That?*, *Kittens! Why Do They Do What They Do?*, and *Puppies! Why Do They Do What They Do?*